"The book about Buddhist humility in which ***you*** *are the hero."*

"A revolutionary approach to maintaining the status quo."

"For people in recovery from the self-help industry."

First Edition. August 2018.

Beating the Conundrums Since 2001

Curved-Space Comedy
A Division of Heavy Meadow Productions
P.O. Box 270156 Louisville, CO 80027-9998 USA

For booking and event information:
www.curvedspacecomedy.com.

ISBN – 978 1 7322 9691 6 – Large Print/5x8
ISBN – 978 1 7322 9690 9 – Pocketbook/4x6
ISBN – 978 1 7322 9692 3 – eBook

Special thanks to Zee Griffler and Michael Hamers for design and graphics support, Timothy Ash, Maurice Smith, Vic Shayne, Bill Pfeiffer, Evan Hodkins, Kristan Olivas, and numerous friends for content support and vetting this material with me, and my parents for mentoring me and encouraging me to write.

"We live vicariously, so you don't have to."

Letting Go Is All We Have To Hold Onto

A Global Philosophical Adventure

"You are what you read."

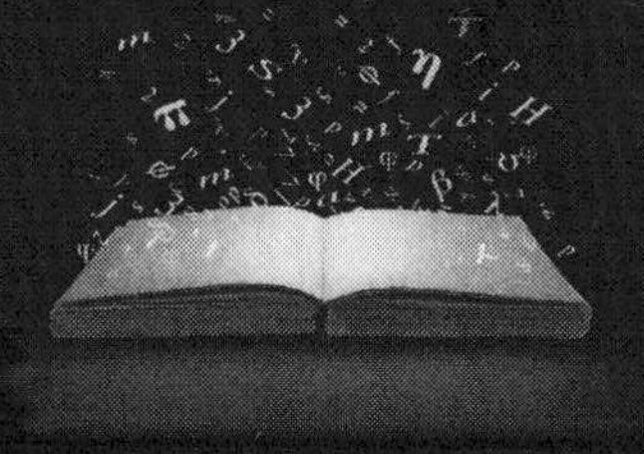

Gregg Eisenberg

TABLE OF CONTENTS

PREFACE

It's rare to find a trifecta of thought streams and modalities as unexpectedly and intimately intertwined as what I have discovered with *The Eisenberg Principles*, presented in the following mind-altering chapters. Here philosophy, physics, and depth psychology marry into uproariously funny vignettes of paradoxical play, each nugget like a piece of deluxe brain-candy which - when unwrapped - is no less serious in its treatment of the human condition as it is absurd. We are not only afforded a chance to glimpse into the thoughts of this wondrously twisted and tantalizing thinker, we are challenged to follow him into the surprising and impossible rabbit holes of language he unearths on every page.

Every aphorism (or *laughorism*) is an exciting odyssey that uses verbal gymnastics to stretch the boundaries of logic and throws the semantics of everyday language into question; each demands something of the reader, but ultimately gives back three times over in disarming humor, fresh insight, and apparent resolution.

A must-read for everyone grappling with the lexicon and linguistics of our age; readers will feel an undeniable sense of homecoming on the pages to follow. The concepts are that sharp, that poignant, and that evolved.

In a society that now literally feels as if it's falling apart at the seams at times, Gregg Eisenberg's book unflinchingly puts us back together again. At least for the duration of the reader's voyage. And maybe with a few frayed edges. Here all of the quizzical quandaries and quirky conundrums of the human condition are laid bare. And we do feel understood, if only for a little while...

If science and medicine can save lives, laughter can save lives, too. Read this book and then give a copy of it to that inquisitive, sensitive (and possibly troubled) person you know who hasn't been laughing enough lately, or whose spirits need to be uplifted, or whose imagination is ready to be expanded simply by engaging with these intelligent calisthenics for the mind.

I am proud to introduce the work of Gregg Eisenberg: the Prince of Paradox, the Jester of Juxtaposition. This book, like Gregg's stage productions Even the Earth is Bipolar and Follow Your Bris, take us from the "comforts of cliché" to the "chasms of contradiction," and entertain us as we stand at the edge of the dark abyss and look across it together.

Kristan Olivas, 2018

INTRODUCTION

The great Austrian philosopher and linguist, **Ludwig Wittgenstein**, once stated:

> *"An entire treatise of philosophy could be written that consists entirely of humor."*

One reason he made this statement is that humor is an excellent vehicle for exposing the cracks and crags in human knowledge that suffer from incongruity or internal contradiction, and holding them up to the light of day for all to see. As we celebrate the 100th anniversaries of relativity and quantum physics, the job of the modern philosopher now runs in parallel with the job of the comedian and scientist: to help us wrap our minds around truths that come in strange packages which are no longer linear and predictable. Scientific truth doesn't fit into tidy packages anymore, and neither does our "human story." We are now forced to embrace paradox, ambiguity, and complexity into our everyday vernacular and figures of speech.

I hope these jokes, known as *The Eisenberg Principles*, will shed light on the contradictions of the human psyche and stir our collective conversation forward. I find many of the accepted linguistic devices and popular idioms that we use to speak about mind, meaning, and the human story unsatisfyingly simplistic. We need to keep digging, friends; we need to continue breaking the conceptual rocks, excavating the emotional terrain, and polishing the rough semantics we rely on to describe and relate to the human condition.

In that regard, I am inspired by the words of the great transcendentalist, **Henry David Thoreau**:

"Be a Columbus to whole new continents and worlds within you, opening new channels, not of trade, but of thought."

Many writers and innovators see this excavation as their life work. When asked why he wrote novels, the Czech author **Franz Kafka** made this statement:

"A book should serve to act like an ice-axe to break the frozen sea within us."

While I am sensing he struggled with winter depression, I do accept his basic premise: if a writer is going to undertake a philosophical inquiry and write about it, they have no choice but to go wherever the material leads them, and break open new conceptual, emotional, and aesthetic ground at all costs. That is what **Norman Mailer** meant when he said: "Whenever I sit down to write, whatever I write has to be more honest and cut to the core more than whatever I wrote last time."

A radio interviewer once asked Grateful Dead guitarist **Jerry Garcia**, "What gets in the way of your creativity the most?" Mr. Garcia's response was:

"Everything I think."

Nothing hinders our understanding of reality more than what we believe we already understand about it. **Stephen Hawking** is said to have said something very similar: "The greatest enemy of knowledge is not ignorance; it is the illusion of knowledge." To learn to question what we already think we know, without throwing away scientific evidence or indulging in fantasy, is one of the challenges of our times.

It is not unlike the philosophy of jazz, expressed well by **Miles Davis** when he said: "Don't play what's there. Play what's not there."

Linear thoughts are the means by which we humans make logical sense of human experience, but reality itself seems to be more and more non-linear. Quantum physicists taught us convincingly that we observers affect our own observations so much that we cannot accurately separate ourselves from what we are trying to observe. As the brilliant **Max Planck** explained:

"Science cannot solve the ultimate mystery of nature, because, in the last analysis, we ourselves are a part of the mystery that we are trying to solve."

It's not easy to "play what's not there." In our haste to have certainty, we often cut corners, compromise on accuracy, or distort subjects. The post-impressionists and cubist painters deliberately focused on these distortions. "Art," said **Picasso**, "is a lie, which helps us realize the truth." Or as I state, later in this book:

"We all have to bend the facts a little in life to compensate for how we distort reality."

According to **Deepok Chokpra**, we have been educated to not think in paradox because of a felt-need for certainty. And author **Gregg Levoy** beautifully describes the intellectual challenge of staying suspended in uncertainty:

"The heroic skill of holding paradox, the endless struggle between two things that are each 100% true and at completely odds with each other, is not some parlor game, or some pose you strike. It is ferocious and dizzying work that you do at the edge of a cliff."

And I couldn't disagree less. The Austrian founder of modern psychology, **Sigmund Freud**, summed it up most succinctly:

"Neurosis itself is the inability to tolerate or cope with ambiguity."

Instead of running away from paradox, we must learn to embrace it; instead of dreading ambiguity and dissonance, we need to become comfortable with them. To quote *The New York Times'* **David Brooks**:

"Wisdom isn't a body of information. It's the moral quality of knowing what you don't know and figuring out a way to

handle your ignorance, uncertainty, and limitation."

And what more palatable way to expose and explore our collective ignorance than through the body of humor. As the German philosopher **Fredrick Nietzsche** wrote:

"We should call any alleged truth 'false' which was not accompanied by hearty laughter."

Laughter itself is a moment of pure epiphany. We laugh when we hear something that unexpectedly shines new light on the familiar. It is good for the brain, and good for several other organs, as well. The Indian philosopher **Osho** concurs:

"The only thing you should take seriously in life are the jokes."

Physicist **Werner Heisenberg**, the father of the Heisenberg Uncertainty Principle - which states that the behavior of even the smallest particles at the fabric of existence is slippery and indeterminate - also understood the paradoxical nature of reality and the important role of humor for coping with it:

"There are things in the Universe that are so serious that you can only joke about them."

Buddhist monks, especially from the Zen tradition, also used humor to elicit moments of epiphany. This entire compendium of aphorisms ("laughorisms") could be regarded as a collection of modern Zen koans, one-sentence expressions of thought that force the mind into a moment of confusion – followed by insight. Perhaps followed once again by a state of confusion.

As you turn through these pages, you will not be alone. There are millions of truth-seekers of all generations who love improvisational music, cubist art, quantum physics, and Buddhist philosophy, who also share the conviction that new conceptual ground needs to be broken to sow the seeds for new language.

The British poet **Rudyard Kipling** wrote:

"Words are, of course, the most powerful drug used by mankind."

And so I use them (words, not drugs) to make this book's important point, which is that most positions are hard to defend, because paradox or uncertainty are never far behind.

"The religion of the future will consist of a catalogue of jokes," my friend **Evan Hodkins** once said. "All humor is philosophy," my other friend, **Vic Shayne**, once said. Letting go is all any of us really has to hold on to. If you can wrap your mind around that mobius strip, dear reader, you are ahead of the pack.

Have a Namaste.

Gregg Eisenberg
Listening to Ornette Coleman, 3:21 AM
Boulder, Colorado

"When we told you that humor can lead to enlightenment, we were *not* joking."

~CHAPTER 1~

Take My Advice And Think For Yourself

"Not only is the Universe stranger than we think, it is stranger than we *can* think."
— Werner Heisenberg

"Mathematics is the subject in which we never know if what we are saying is true."
— Bertrand Russell

"I can verify with 100% certainty that I don't have a clue what I'm talking about."
— Gregg Eisenberg

The best way to focus on the moment is to sit back, think about where you want to end up, and work backwards from there.

We were practicing Zen when the identity theft happened, which is why they didn't really get much.

Aristotle said "We are what we repeatedly do," a thought I often ponder on my way to the bathroom.

I always follow my instincts, except when
I get a funny feeling maybe I shouldn't.

I do believe in a completely parallel
Universe, I just don't think we're going
to run into it any time soon.

I like to learn from all people,
but especially from those who agree with me.

The rest of us think you're being totally
paranoid for feeling singled out by the group.

❂

Unlike you, I am not drawing distinctions
between us.

❂

The people who say
"you create your reality with your thoughts"
sure are hard to get away from at parties.

I do agree with Plato: To thine own self be true; but not necessarily about everything. And certainly not all at once.

I am totally irreverent, but only out of deep respect for everything that's sacred.

I love that you are such a free spirit, and I want you to be mine forever.

Less really is more, so the more less you can get, the better!

Focusing on quality over quantity does eventually work, if you do it enough times.

The principles of polarity are not that great, but they don't suck either.

Now that I have it all, I miss the feeling that there must be something more.

I need to take a little break from creating a lifestyle I don't need a vacation from.

I'm making a detailed list of all the things in life I'd rather not remember.

I still haven't wrapped my mind around the
idea that thoughts can't describe reality.

I am finally transcending my need to be
constantly rising to new levels.

The pursuit of fame is said to be pure vanity
by some of the most prestigious
members of our society.

I'm an old soul, but I'm also a late riser,
so it all evens out.

You, of all people, need to stop
taking things so personally!

I hate the stupid, petty power struggles
in which I don't have the upper hand.

I feel so sorry for you that everyone
thinks of you as a victim.

Life may be terribly hard and very lonely,
but at least we are living longer these days.

❂

Most problems are completely imaginary,
and for some people this is a very real issue!

❂

I want to make my big difference
in the world by showing people that
things never really change.

Dualism does work for me,
but only about half the time.

I both can and cannot hold opposing ideas
in my mind at the same time.

The truth that set me free
cost me everything I have.

By refusing to compete with you,
I have already won.

I'm giving you quite a bit more
unconditional love than you deserve.

This whole human experience is merely
a long, lucid dream, and in it
you still owe me 200 bucks!

I question everything people say, but only
because that's what the last
guy told me to do.

People are hungry for very simplistic
explanations, and that's all you really
need to know.

I'm just blindly going along with the plan for
us to not act like a bunch of sheep.

EPILOGUE

Reptile brain says "Kill!"
Mammal brain says "See if
empathy will work first!"
Neo-cortex says "Tape-record
the conversation and
establish a paper trail."

~CHAPTER 2~

Real Space Has Curves

"Jews don't drink much because it interferes with their suffering."
— Milton Berle

"One's real life is often the life one does not lead."
— Oscar Wilde

"I would offer to be there with you in spirit, but I have a prior commitment."
— Gregg Eisenberg

The best way to stop looking for yourself is
probably just around the next corner.

I'm feeling fine, which is simply
a rough average between
devastated and ecstatic.

I started to party on Wednesday this week,
just to take some pressure off the weekend.

Either there will be a way out of binary
language traps or there won't be.

Living in a radically paradoxical universe
has been nothing but a complete blessing.

God only knows
if I will use my free will *this* time.

Nihilists claim we can't know anything;
I don't even think we know *that*!

⊛

Does having too many options make you feel
happy, sad, burdened, angry, or irritable?

⊛

I feel deep gratitude for all the ways
positive thinking helped me win my
lawsuit against my kids.

My notes about entropy are getting
more and more disorganized everyday.

The people who believe in mind over matter
are running straight at us
with large sticks in their hands.

Once I made peace with the irony in life,
everything else became harder to bear.

The impossibility of uncovering the truth
has finally been exposed to the light of day.

⊛

There are countless things you just know
without putting them into words
(but I couldn't tell you what they are.)

⊛

I am borrowing from the future
to pay for the past, but I'm staying very
present in the process.

I totally resent your self-indulgent lifestyle,
and hope it rubs off on me
as soon as possible.

How can I tell you to get the hell away
from me if you won't come any closer?

I would give you my undivided attention, but
I feel it would be rude
to the person I'm texting with.

The contradictions in life drive me crazy,
but for some reason the paradoxes
don't bother me a bit.

Reasoning is over-rated, but
it takes a while to figure that out.

I am someone who is non-dogmatic
just as a matter of personal principle.

My inability to feel my emotions
is tearing my stomach apart.

If only we had it a little worse,
we'd realize how good things are.

❂

At the very least, we can say we didn't cling
on to the silver linings.

❂

Youth is wasted on the young,
but prolonged adolescence
is wasted on the adults.

I have experienced deep self-knowledge
many times, but only vicariously.

My Shadow Self tends to grow longer in the
late afternoon, usually around sunset.

Is it just my imagination,
or am I making things up?

Being able to grasp our mortal insignificance
really puts humans on the cosmic map.

❁

We don't need to look beyond our own
minds to find the possibility of meaning
(but we might need to look away
from our phones for a minute.)

❁

The digital database of all human knowledge
isn't the only thing he's held in the palm of
his hand lately.

The way a song “has” a melody is not the
same as the way a car “has” the color red or
the way my wife “has” irritable
bowel syndrome.

I keep repeating under my breath:
I don’t need affirmations,
I don’t need affirmations…

I am not my thoughts, I am not this body,
and frankly I’m not very employable.

This is a real opportunity to do things
the same way we've always done them before.

⊛

I'm trying to model the behavior
of not conforming to example
for others.

⊛

The concept that there is no universal
cohesion seems to be the only
theory that holds together.

EPILOGUE

I spent half my life struggling
to attain golden ideals,
and the other half trying to
accept life's imperfections;
the rest of the time I just relaxed.

~CHAPTER 3~

Even The Earth Is Bipolar

"The average man, who does not know what to do with this life, wants another one which shall last forever."
— Anatole France

"The sign of a first-rate intelligence is the ability to hold two opposing ideas in the mind at the same time, and still retain the ability to function."
— F. Scott Fitzgerald

"The world would be more tolerant of differences if everyone were more like me."
— Gregg Eisenberg

You really only get what you pay for in life,
if you want my two cents.

⊛

For a small fee, we tell you that you can do
great things; for a large fee,
we say you can do anything.

⊛

There is a lot of work you need to do on
yourself before you can realize
you're fine the way you are.

Those most eager to be seen as well-adjusted
can usually be counted on
to do the most insane things.

❁

I saw the Universe in a grain of sand about
ten minutes before the police picked me up.

❁

I am giddy with incredible joy that you are
back on your bipolar medication.

I'm your Prince Charming,
come to set you free
(and take you home to my mother.)

Other than how it compromises my sanity,
I think our relationship is pretty healthy.

I would pay you to break my heart, but
it looks like you'll do it for free.

Lao-tzu believed: "The truth that can be spoken of is not the eternal truth," which explains why he was so quiet at parties.

Out beyond ideas of right-doing and wrong-doing, wrote Rumi, there is a field; I will rob you there.

Look for the truth within, friends; it's a lot cheaper than airfare to Asia.

I don't compare myself to others nearly as much as some people do.

Inner peace is available;
you just have to go out there and grab it.

My identity crisis is clearly
what my life is all about.

My parents raised me to live free of guilt,
and for that I'm deeply indebted.

We never show favortism to any of our
children; our middle child
wouldn't stand for it!

I'm very concerned about my mother; she
hasn't worried about me in two weeks.

I keep losing sight of the fact
that everything is fleeting.

My first reflex upon hearing you is to suggest you stop being so robotic in your responses.

I'm extremely patient and loving with everyone, up to the point someone gets on my nerves.

If only things had gone wrong earlier, we wouldn't *be* in this predicament!

We've arrived at that historic moment,
predicted long ago, when we would lose
all interest in ancient prophecies.

❁

We've got to make rejecting the status quo
the new norm!

❁

We owe it to future generations
to cut all ties with the past.

Life is shockingly unfair (which has worked to my advantage most of the time.)

A couple acts of altruism would really lift my spirits right about now.

Some people just aren't lucky enough to appreciate how incredibly fortunate they are.

I'm too busy figuring out
the patterns in the data
to know what's really going on.

Your premature reactions are welcome here,
but just a little bit later.

I'm a pretty nice guy,
especially for someone like me.

Succumbing to peer pressure
is seriously frowned upon around here.

❂

We live in a probablistic universe, and it's
very unlikely we can do anything about it.

❂

Accepting there are no panaceas in life
actually solved all my problems.

There is absolutely no honor in trying to
defend your dignity for anything more
than four hours per day.

As you get older, you get clearer about
what's really transpiring around you,
but aside from that it's an enjoyable process.

I look forward to finally removing
100% of the unrealistic expectations
I place on myself.

EPILOGUE

There's what you possess in one hand,
and what you lack in the other;
being the owner of both,
you are free to choose
which to obsess on.

~CHAPTER 4~

Just Say "No" To Your Resistance

"The past isn't dead; it isn't even past."
— William Faulkner

"The efforts we make to escape from our destiny only serve to lead us into it."
— Ralph Waldo Emerson

"It just wasn't my fate to become the person I was always destined to be."
— Gregg Eisenberg

The Dalai Lama insists that "Your enemy is your greatest teacher," which is why I now carry mace at school.

I realized the biological fight against entropy is futile today, and that was even before recess.

When I was young I decided not to base my self-worth on my income-level, which was a costly mistake.

I was thoroughly indoctrinated as a child to resist all forms of thought control.

We're all suddenly trying to break free of herd mentality at the same time.

I want to go back to the good, old days when I couldn't appreciate how good I had it.

We're all stuck in the prisons of our minds,
but at least we get three hot meals a day here.

I've been outside of the box for four days
now, and I'm thinking pretty damn hard.

I reached out and touched someone;
what are you in for?

I am so much more than just
a guy sitting here stripping away
his delusions of grandeur.

When I see how little progress
I've made in my Buddhist practice lately,
I feel emptiness inside.

I'm clearly headed straight towards having
no direction in life.

Being on the cutting edge of cultural change
is coming back into vogue these days.

I bought everything I need for the revolution
at Walmart; and it was all on clearance.

The big industrial war machine gave me
another quiet morning in the jacuzzi.

I used to live in the present moment,
and plan to get back there again soon.

I now only have about three minutes left
to learn how to manage my time better.

The concept of diminishing returns
keeps getting more important every day.

To rid oneself of useless thoughts, one must
first study the function, purpose, and
history of thinking.

I don't have a path, which makes it a lot easier to stay on track.

⊛

You alone are in control of your own destiny (along with about 400 other people.)

⊛

If I were you, I'd be a lot more like me.

Just being born, we've already won
the greatest lottery of all, but the odds of
realizing this are extremely slim.

I hope you're not thinking
what I'm not thinking.

I find it fascinating that you think of me
as self-absorbed.

If I were the ideal version of myself,
I wouldn't try to be perfect.

We're all one, but some of us are
a bit more one than others.

Nanotechnology is the next big thing.

Each of us needs to learn how to stop taking things so personally in our very own idiosyncratic way.

❂

Shoot for the stars, follow your dreams, and *stop* being such an overachiever.

❂

If you weren't going anywhere, you'd be there by now.

The only solid advice I have to give
is about what things *not* to do in life.

❁

I have no doubt that people
all over the world mean the same thing
when they use the word "projection".

❁

I truly look up to all people who see
everyone as their equal.

Here's a 30,000-year old legacy
of language, culture, and instincts;
Now, think for yourself!

Living a life that isn't
personally challenging me
really tests my patience.

You are a terrible listener, but
I bet you hear that all the time.

EPILOGUE

I used to think I was making
something out of life;
then I thought life was
making something out of me.
Now, I'm hoping for either.

~CHAPTER 5~

Immediate Gratification Is Worth Waiting For

**"In this world there are only two tragedies:
One is not getting what one wants,
and the other is getting it."**
— Oscar Wilde

**"A comic jest often decides matters of
importance more effectually
than serious statements."**
— Horace

**"Discovering that free will is a total illusion
actually opened up a lot of options for me."**
— Gregg Eisenberg

Tich Nhat Han said "Buddhism teaches us not to run away from suffering," but what about from the IRS?

I know I told you yesterday to stop living in the future, but now it's today, so can we *please* stop living in the past?

The idea of ownership is a complete myth (but you should still hang on to your receipts.)

I don't have anywhere near enough free time to enjoy the incredible abundance of my life.

Eckhart Tolle is correct: Only the present moment is real (but it compounds by the hour and accrues at midnight.)

I'm a free spirit, but I'm raising my rates soon.

Smarter gun laws would sure trigger some
great changes in our society.

⊛

Please don't reduce a mid-20s, east-Bay,
pro-choice progressive like me to your
simplistic labels.

⊛

If you think the human spirit will
succumb to despair,
your position is hopeless.

Wanting English to be the official language is a real zeitgeist of the times; and it's all but a *fait accompli.*

⊛

There's a global conspiracy trying to make us believe only a few people control the world.

⊛

I'm quite young at heart;
it's my kidney that could use a break.

Facebook is the perfect tool to destroy the dominant paradigm, while helping its shareholders, too.

Life is not a popularity contest; if you agree, please like, comment, and share.

Big Brother isn't watching me, at least that's what my Google searches are showing.

Empathy has allowed us to succeed so prodigiously as a species, we're on the brink of extinction.

Humans tend to imagine there's a lot of intention to the Universe, but that's just part of the plan.

I never could have escaped the delusion of separation without you.

My search for truth came to an abrupt end
when I realized there is no finality.

It takes many years of deep reflection
to realize that wisdom is not the goal in life.

⊛

The concept that "everything is perfect"
could use a little fine-tuning.

⊛

I never got the memo telling me
that I'm supposed to think for myself.

I don't allow complete strangers on the street to verbally abuse me; that's reserved for the folks who love me most.

❁

I learned how to feel shitty about myself
from some of the best people
you could ever meet.

❁

I'm gonna go way out on a limb and say the apple doesn't fall far from the tree.

We all cling to the stories about the world
that most comfort us, which
greatly disturbs me.

William James basically proved that we can
never know the "objective truth", but
I *still* hate being wrong.

The fact that we weren't working with any
clues was right under our nose
the entire time.

I am utterly devastated by
the total lack of drama in my life.

My natural air of sincerity invites others to
be genuine too, especially when
I lay it on thick.

If you don't believe I'm an introvert, you can
ask my 20 best friends.

I never learned all that much from suffering
that I didn't pretty much already know.

❁

I'm now trying to compensate
for all the years I spent believing
I could make up for lost time later.

❁

It takes a lifetime of practice
to learn how to make things feel
like they're happening for the first time.

Kindness is the universal answer, friends; please don't annoy me with your personal questions.

❁

You know love is the ultimate goal of human evolution because *you* know every damn thing.

❁

If you haven't learned to feel compassion for all living beings, your life has been a total waste of resources.

Genetic destiny dealt me a hard blow the other day, but I'm back on my own four paws.

❁

I'm the black sheep in my family; I'm the only one who's comfortable in groups.

❁

I just can't get used to the idea that evolution is based on the ability to adapt.

EPILOGUE

I am not my body,
I am not the sum of
my accomplishments,
I am not what other
people think of me, and I
find all of this *very* uplifting.

~CHAPTER 6~

Feeling Insufficient Just Isn't Good Enough

"The ultimate result of shielding men
effects of folly is to fill the world wi
— Herbert

"The means by which certain ple
gained bring pains m
greater the
—

"If you zoom out f
you'll see you waste
trying to see the bigg
— Gregg

Freud asserted "Neurosis *is* the inability
to cope with ambiguity,"
but the research is so bloody inconclusive!

My id and superego are arguing again,
while everyone else is just ignoring *me*.

Just give me an electric shock every time
I succumb to behavioral conditioning.

I can accept the laws of thermo-dynamics,
but I've got to do it on my own terms.

I go in and out of understanding that
photons can behave like waves or particles.

Once I discovered the principles of
randomness, everything in my life
fell into place.

I am right on the cusp of accepting
that there's nowhere further to go.

I learned how to stop mimicking the
behavior of others from the best.

I'm only using 5% of my brain's
mental capacity, but that's ok,
I'm only taking out the garbage.

The first step on the road to achieving unlimited freedom is getting total control of your mind.

If everything you do is slavishly serving the question "Am I good enough?", then I have some bad news for you...

I'm choosing an unconscious lifestyle for a number of specific, powerful reasons.

There are a thousand different ways to say it:
Language is too limiting!

⊛

If we didn't feel so lonely, we might not be so happy to see each other.

⊛

I just wasn't mature enough to appreciate the blessings of my early toddler years.

Nothing cured my narcissism better than a good long look in the mirror.

I'm practicing minimalism less and less
every year.

As soon as you stop being so superstitious,
your income will double.

I got the suffering over with early in life;
now I'm working through the debt.

The polls are telling us to ignore what the surveys and focus groups are saying.

⊛

We live in a society that is stuck in egotistical over-drive, and I wanna know what you're gonna do about it!

⊛

Don't blame me! I only support locally-owned multi-national petrochemical companies.

Sometimes I ask myself,
how would a highly-intelligent Neanderthal
handle this situation.

I'm finally in possession of myself;
now I'm trying to get possession of my car.

The spiritual warrior in me subdues my
fierce anger and lovingly transforms it
into petty resentment.

If you don't stop feeling so responsible for everyone's feelings, you're gonna bring the whole group down.

⊛

I love shared experiences, especially when someone else picks up the tab.

⊛

You're lucky I'm only being passive-aggressive right now.

I would travel the seven seas to get away
from being another washed-up cliché.

⊛

I need a good ghost-writer to help me
describe all the skeletons in my closet.

⊛

The stars are now in perfect alignment
for me to break my addiction
to magical thinking.

If you were just a little different,
you wouldn't need to change at all.

Nothing helped me stop looking back
so much as past life regressions.

I've made a full-time job
out of getting over myself.

EPILOGUE

You don't *need* to be enlightened;
you just need to be
a little larger than
your disappointments.

~CHAPTER 7~

Never Stop Trying
To Surrender

"As far as the properties of mathematics refer to reality, they are not certain; and as far as they are certain, they do not refer to reality."
— Albert Einstein

"How wonderful that we have met with paradox. Now we have some hope of making progress."
— Niels Bohr

"If we could break our addiction to Hollywood endings, we would all live happily ever after."
— Gregg Eisenberg

Being less ego-oriented gives you a slight advantage over other people.

I will humbly bow down to anyone who admits that I'm better than they are.

The Dalai Lama teaches that "Desire is the root problem," but *I* think it's not getting what you want.

Once Isaac Newton figured out the rules of calculus, the equation for gravity hit him like a ton of bricks.

Pretending the principles of math don't matter only compounded my problems.

I'm sorry for going outside the lines of Euclidean geometry to prove my point.

My big plan for the future is to
let go of the past.

⊛

Ram Dass advises us to "be here now"
(it sure beats processing your childhood.)

⊛

We ought to enjoy being free from the
pressures of time now,
while we still have a chance.

Nothing freed my mind more than
radically limiting my options.

I wasted a lot of valuable time in life thinking
I need to make every day count.

If I am not against myself,
who will be against me?

I'm trying to get better
at not raising the bar on myself
every few months.

It just hit me that I keep having the same
monumental breakthroughs
over and over again.

Realizing I won't achieve
enlightenment in this lifetime
shattered my ego into a thousand pieces.

The brain fires logarithmically,
the mind thinks exponentially, and my
retirement fund was grown hydroponically.

❂

The feeling of normalcy hits me
in the strangest of places.

❂

I'm the poster child
for people who don't fit into any category.

There are things the human mind can never accept, and you just have to get used to it.

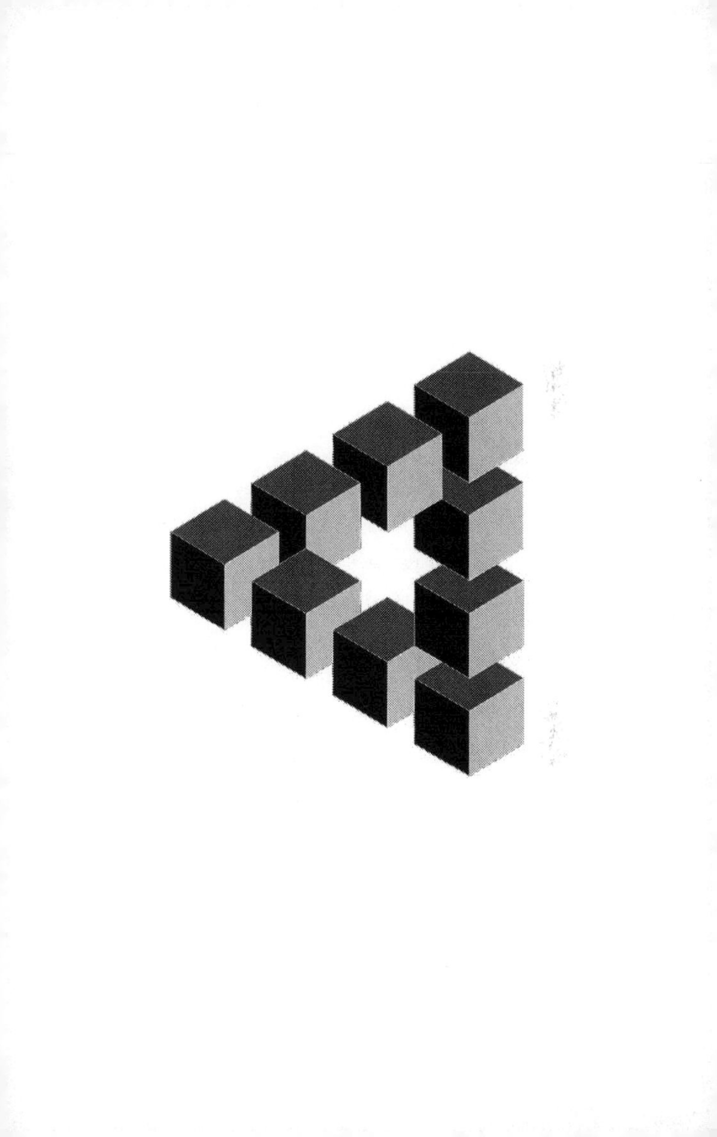

I am *not* multi-tasking:
I'm doing one thing at a time
in two-second intervals.

I'm sorry I wasn't totally focused on the
present moment about 45 minutes ago.

I was trying to be a good listener,
but you kept interrupting me.

It took me 20 years of thinking
to finally figure out
that my mind moves way too quickly.

That meditation retreat was so bad,
I wish I'd stayed home
and done nothing instead.

If ever there was a moment when the
concept of time was just an illusion,
it's right now.

We are so much more than just the chemical
reactions in our brains; we're also
a bunch of muscular reflexes.

I have a Freudian-like resistance
to all early 20th century dogma.

My brain is racked in cognitive dissonance,
and I say that with a mixture
of pride and shame.

The Buddhist concept that "thinking is the problem" must always be kept at the forefront of your mind.

My ability to grasp the empty nature of reality just vanished into thin air.

I will be able to experience the non-duality of the cosmos a lot easier when you leave the room.

I need to stop repeating the same
stories in my head, I tell myself
every night at bedtime.

I'll share with you the secrets of the leisure
life once I get a few minutes to spare.

I'm so eager to show you I'm right,
I'll bend the truth to prove it.

There's no place like
just a little further over there.

⊛

Embracing radical simplicity
improved my life on 18 different levels.

⊛

Pain is inevitable, suffering is optional,
and tonight we have a Malbec
that pairs well with both.

EPILOGUE

Nietzsche said "It is precisely the truth,
stated in a bold, new way,
that *is* the essence of humor,"
but then his appendix burst,
his wife died,
and he wrote *The Will to Power*.

~CHAPTER 8~

Think Of Me When You're Meditating

"Acting is all about honesty;
if you can fake that, you've got it made."
— George Burns

"Life is far too important to be taken seriously."
— Oscar Wilde

"I am cleverly disguised as someone
not wearing a costume."
— Gregg Eisenberg

I like to appear informed about the world,
but I don't really want to know
what's going on.

If the suffering of humanity doesn't make
you weep like a baby, then you're
no man at all!

I compensate for being a superhero at night
by sleeping 'til noon most days.

I have a terrible memory:
I can't forget anything.

In my quest to conquer obsessive-compulsive
disorder, I left no stone unturned.

It took a lot of failure to get
where I am today.

I want to genuinely apologize now
for how insincere I'll turn out to be later.

I admit I have a little problem with vanity,
but aside from that I have so many
other good qualities!

Once I stopped pursuing the truth, it started
stalking me at night.

Most of the things
I worried about never came to pass;
it was the things I never saw coming...

Today is the first day of the rest of your
30-year mortgage.

Can we all at least agree that
the idea of consensus reality
is just an illusion?

I always figured a little false humility
is better than *no* humility at all.

I'm willing to feel genuine remorse
for what I did, if that's what
gets me off the hook.

I'm a great listener:
I love to hear myself talk.

Every couple hours I catch myself
wondering what it would be like to be
free of intrusive thoughts.

My personal story is just an illusion,
my ego is just an abstraction,
and my criminal record is fictitious.

I saw the light driving home last night;
in fact, there were several,
and they weren't white.

The crucial premise underlying my entire philosophy is that there are no valid points of departure.

I’ve abandoned my formulas for happiness,
but who knows? Maybe randomness will
work better.

I’ve noticed I wobble a lot in my beliefs,
and you know what? I’m not sure *how* I feel
about that.

A human lifespan is so short;
the Universe had better get to know us now.

I am a holographic mirror of the Cosmos, looking at the moment for a good deal on snow tires.

The concept that "we're all connected" started having greater appeal once I began the bankruptcy process.

I stopped neurotically clinging to the past at 1:47 PM on January 14, 2008.

I've been focusing on my
attention-deficit disorder
for 12 years straight.

Learning how to think more abstractly
is now at the top of my bucket list.

There's a 50-50 chance that
I'll probably be wrong.

Once we liberate ourselves from the myth of emancipation, we'll finally be free.

⊛

There is no separate "I" behind my thoughts; at least that's how it seems to *me*.

⊛

I am not living "in" this body,
though I make a pretty good living "off" it.

There must be more to life than
always wondering what else is out there.

❂

If you don't know how good you've got it,
then you don't got it so good.

❂

I'm not doing much to alleviate the suffering
of humanity, other than
transferring some of mine onto you.

Expressing my individuality is more
important to me than being validated
by the group (and people just *love* that!)

You just look like the kind of guy
who would judge a book by its cover.

First I need to get my parking ticket
validated, then I need you
to tell me I'm alright.

EPILOGUE

Dr. Wayne Dyer used to say,
"If you want to change your life,
change your mind",
and I've been going
back and forth
on that one for a while.

~CHAPTER 9~

Non-Attachment Is Addictive

"The limits of my language are the limits of my mind. All I know is what I have words for."
— Ludwig Wittgenstein

"A mathematician who is not also something of a poet will never be a complete mathematician."
— Bertrand Russell

"If you appreciate my sincerity, I'll be sure to mention your good taste to the others."
— Gregg Eisenberg

We don't have to be in the same room
to feel the love we share; in fact,
it's better if we aren't.

We're all moving forward as one to the same
destination: we're just taking two-billion cars
to get there.

I want to see myself as a loving person,
but you get in my way.

Breaking your addiction to repetitive habits
requires a daily practice.

If you aren't someone who can
"fake it 'til you make it,"
just pretend that you are.

There's only so far I'd go to curry favor with
others (and it's pretty damn far.)

There is an endless chorus of voices
in my head telling me to quiet my mind.

❁

Since I stopped watching the clock, I've loved
every minute of my life.

❁

Last week I was feeling one with the
Universe, but this week barely even
the Solar System.

A life without comparisons is actually much better than the alternative.

When you meet a man
who thinks for himself,
follow in his footsteps.

I'm still waiting for the ideal moment to accept life's imperfections.

The concept of infinity is 100% fictitious
(but it has endless intrigue.)

I know absolutely nothing about science,
and about math even less.

I am utterly resigned to the fact that
the future is wide open.

When I first set off down
the road of modesty, I had no idea
I would take it so far.

I was truly saddened to share the news of
your misfortune with all of my friends.

I learned how to sit really still
in India, China, and Japan.

It's normal to struggle with existential issues
while you're still alive,
but they say it gets even worse later.

I'll do better at
remaining "detatched about outcomes"
when things start improving.

❁

I'm just sitting here quietly breathing and meditating on my future income potential.

❁

Divorcing yourself from materialism is the best value proposition in the market today.

Our finally learning how to live without
anticipating the future has only just begun.

Not realizing you have "good problems"
is actually a very serious condition.

We better learn how to relax soon,
because time is quickly running out.

You've got to know how to argue
both sides of an argument –
there's no two ways about it!

That which didn't kill me also
didn't do wonders for my first marriage.

I feel very sorry for anyone
who stands between me
and a more gentle way of living.

"Learn to love the questions," Ranier Rilke
advises (because the answers
are usually distressing.)

Instead of me going through the drama of
"losing it all" to realize how good I've got it,
could I just start with half?

I am way too easily distracted by life's
most pressing, fundamental problems.

EPILOGUE

My entire purpose in this moment
is to simply wipe the counter,
squeeze the sponge over the sink,
and stop thinking about
the end of civilization.

~CHAPTER 10~

I Love What I Don't Know About You So Far

"When people are free to do as they please, they usually imitate each other."
— Eric Hoffer

"I always wanted to be somebody, but now I realize I should have been more specific."
— Lily Tomlin

"Scarcity isn't the real problem, but far too few of us realize this!"
— Gregg Eisenberg

When I'm feeling overwhelmed by too many
choices, I like to stay home and
browse the internet.

Everything in modern philosophy is
pointing towards a place that exists
far beyond spatial metaphors.

Now that I've walked a few miles
in my own shoes, I can tell you this:
I'm not who I thought I was.

Byron Katie teaches us to "not believe everything we think," and there's not a doubt in my mind she's correct!

⊛

Rumi counseled us to "Gamble away both worlds for love," not both condos.

⊛

Life is hard,
but it does come with free,
round-trip flights around the Sun.

Adam Smith's "invisible hand of the free market" just showed me its middle finger again.

Survival of the fittest is an idea that will eventually lose in the marketplace of ideas.

Thanks to the fickle finger of fate, I found out my prostate is okay.

I will ultimately take a rational path,
but not before I'm certain
being impulsive won't work first.

"'To be true, a statement must have internal
consistency' is always true"
is not always valid.

I'm a theoretical physicist,
but I'm an actual bus driver.

I wouldn't be who I am today
if it weren't for your influence
(but I forgive you.)

We felt so good about not having one kid,
we decided to not have a second one
right away.

I found out a mere moment too late
that timing isn't everything.

The way you overreact to other people's
little quirks drives me batshit crazy.

⊛

It's never too late to admit you are someone
who runs behind schedule.

⊛

In the end we'll wish we did less taking
from others, more giving to charity,
and put a can opener in the bomb shelter.

I stopped believing in circular logic when I realized everything happens for a reason.

I feel extremely fortunate to be among
the 10% who don't sit around all day
counting their blessings.

I have stopped taking all metaphysical cues
from people who thought the world is flat.

When I want to learn more about curved
space, I go straight to the library.

I have never allowed anyone
to be controlled by me.

I think I'll procrastinate now and
get it over with.

Have you been taking notes on how much
less self-absorbed I've been lately?

Human consciousness is not expanding, and
I'm becoming more and more
aware of that every day.

I'm an indigo child of the Universe,
a green citizen of the Earth,
and a platinum member of Sam's Club.

Exercising my free will
cost me $400 last night.

It's gonna be a long week at work:
they put me on the paradigm shift.

⊛

I hate being self-employed: the staff is lazy
and the management sucks.

⊛

I got lost following my bliss; then
the IRS found me.

EPILOGUE

Feeling torn between multiple emotions
is a trademark human experience,
and there's really only
one way to feel about that.

~CHAPTER 11~

I'm Going Aggressively New Age

"The first principle is that you must not fool yourself, and you are the easiest person to fool."
— Richard P. Feynman

"I never know how much of what I say is true."
— Bette Midler

"I honestly don't tend to be in denial about my flaws, though I'm sure I must have some."
— Gregg Eisenberg

If I were unaware of how certain experiences could be improved, I'd probably enjoy them more just the way they are.

Life is really a long test
to see how well we can remember
that no one is grading us.

Greed is the one seven deadly sin
I just can't seem to get enough of.

I said I wanted to be a fireman when I grew up; I don't know
where this snoring came from.

The Universe always supports my highest growth; now if only I could support my kids.

My thoughts are thinking me
more than I am thinking them,
but it's my wife who calls the shots.

It's not my delusions of separation
that keep us apart, it's yours.

I fully expected to be dissapointed,
and you didn't let me down one bit.

Please don't take my intolerance
for people like you personally.

Creating a society which encourages unlimited freedom is what we must all focus on now, to the exclusion of all else!

Winning friends by appealing to their vanity is no tactic for someone as fascinating as you.

After feeling connected with the Universe for so long, I'm looking to rent a one-room studio for a while.

I read motivational quotes every 15 minutes
to be reassured I'm not just
hanging by a thread.

I'm putting on a big act that your
fake persona isn't bothering me.

I really don't have a handle on how I first
lost my grip.

I have low levels of cholesterol,
average levels of body fat,
and past-life trauma up the yin-yang.

⊛

The truth is within alright,
sliding around the bacteria in your stomach
and the wall of your large intestine.

⊛

It's easier for a man to move mountains
than to change his character,
but all *I'm* looking for
is a Bud Light and a bathroom.

Einstein waited many years for his wife to
give him a divorce, and that's when
he realized, time itself can slow down.

Rik = 0

Consciousness has really come a long way
since we took the Neanderthal's land
and invented pasta.

Michelangelo said "You keep sculpting until
there isn't anything more to take away",
and I have nothing to add to that.

Europeans think Americans are ill-informed,
loud, and self-centered, but that's so unfair!
We aren't *that* loud.

I'm grieving this week over how much time
I've spent being preoccupied with loss.

⊛

Embracing a secular world-view was one of
the great miracles of my life.

⊛

I am determined to be less goal-oriented
within three months.

I'd love to see the world, but I think I'll stay home and expand my horizons instead.

Once you finally let go of your preferences, things will start to go your way!

I'm celebrating how much freedom of choice I have (because it's about the only option available to me at this point.)

I am 99% objective about everything,
except for how my mind distorts fractions.

⊛

Honey "is" sweet in a different way than
the dog "is" in the yard or the way
my son "is" back on juvenile probation.

⊛

Selective memory worked well for me
five out of five times last week.

EPILOGUE

I'm not interested
in where you went to school,
what you do for a living,
or your annual salary;
I'm interested in how much
cash you're carrying right now.

~CHAPTER 12~

Chop Wood
Carry Water
Charge Phone

"Everything we call *real* is made of things
that cannot be regarded as real."
— Niels Bohr

"Man is equally incapable of seeing
the nothingness from which he emerges
and the infinity in which he is engulfed."
— Blaise Pascal

"I don't want to frivolously worry over
petty details when I could be obsessing
over things that really matter."
— Gregg Eisenberg

I've been extremely preoccupied with
clearing my mind lately.

Even my image consultant is telling me to
stop being so superficial with everyone.

If we can't slow down any faster than *this*,
we'll never relax.

If only I had a little less potential, I could achieve more of my goals.

The new mantra I now repeat is:
"Never say the same thing twice".

It's my own damn fault I screwed up by judging myself so harshly.

I can totally understand what you are saying;
I'm the one I can't understand.

You are borrowing the Earth from entire
future generations; I am borrowing
your identity for only an hour.

I would *never* condemn other people's ways
like you do!

I hate to shatter
your whole Buddhist identity
but there *is* no such thing as ego dissolution.

Through a lengthy process of elimination,
I concluded there's no place like home.

Once you accept the fact that you can never
change your core personality,
you'll never be the same.

I’m under a lot of pressure to lower my stress levels this week.

One must always do one’s absolute best not to try too hard in life.

I’m looking for a new life coach: No experience necessary.

Expecting equal reciprocity from others
is seldom a profitable endeavor.

People who think I am harsh are cowards
projecting their self-esteem issues onto me.

Your personal inadequacies excite me
a whole lot more than mine do.

I have seen the future of Cartesian dualism,
and I can tell you this: it's not all good.

Not only do I believe in being totally
open-minded, I can't tolerate any other way.

I hate drama so much that I immediately
point my finger at those who create it.

If I were really being 100% authentic,
you'd probably ask me to leave the room.

There are more neural connections in my 4-lb. brain than there are stars in a 1000 galaxies, but I *still* bet on the Cubs.

I am not nearly as nostalgic as I used to be a long, long time ago…

This is actually the ideal moment to stop searching for perfection.

We all feel isolated and alone
in the vast web of our total interconnection.

I'm finally getting more aggressive
about my meditation practice.

I'm both manic and depressive,
but I've struck a very healthy balance
between the two.

How you perceive me ultimately depends on you; all I can do is try to manipulate the process.

⊛

I can't believe I'm only 39 years old and I already lie about my age.

⊛

The spirit of non-attachment sure is hard to hold on to.

EPILOGUE

It's a real sign of intelligence to grasp
multiple sides of a complex issue,
try to reconcile them in your mind,
and then feel hopeless
and start to panic.

~CHAPTER 13~

Ambivalence Is The Only Way Forward!

"There is no present or future, only the past, happening over and over again, now."
— Eugene O'Neill

"Unless we lose ourselves, there is no hope of finding ourselves."
— Henry Miller

"If you're not completely baffled by how we got here, you don't understand a lick of world history."
— Gregg Eisenberg

I only care about three things:
money, power,
and the salvation of all living beings.

I'm still waiting for my big break to come
along that proves I'm not just
a victim of circumstance.

I experience a lot of
cognitive dissonance in life,
but it's all good.

The pressure to think outside the box
is starting to close in on me.

⊛

We are right on the verge of realizing that
things are about to stay the same.

⊛

The pretenses you've absorbed to thrive
in your part of society bother me
a lot more than mine.

Taking my unsolicited advice
is something I would not recommend,
even if no one asked me.

I found sobriety so addictive,
I abstained from it for a month.

You'll stop believing
satisfaction is always around the next corner
in just a little while from now.

The Universe expanded 115 trillion miles
in the time it took me to decide
which shoes to wear today.

We should all be wandering around much
more care-free, because any of us could get
slammed by a bus tomorrow.

I knew it was my fault that
the inevitable happened.

Experience has taught me that I don't learn all that much from what happens.

My inner witness has come to testify against me again.

If it bothers you so much that I'm being a martyr, why don't you just crucify me!

I don't go around worrying about how other people see me; it just wouldn't look good.

⊛

Your annoying habits make it impossible for me to unconditionally love you.

⊛

I am very uncomfortable
being the center of attention
for more than two hours at a time.

I just don't have anywhere to put the idea
that the Universe is mostly empty space.

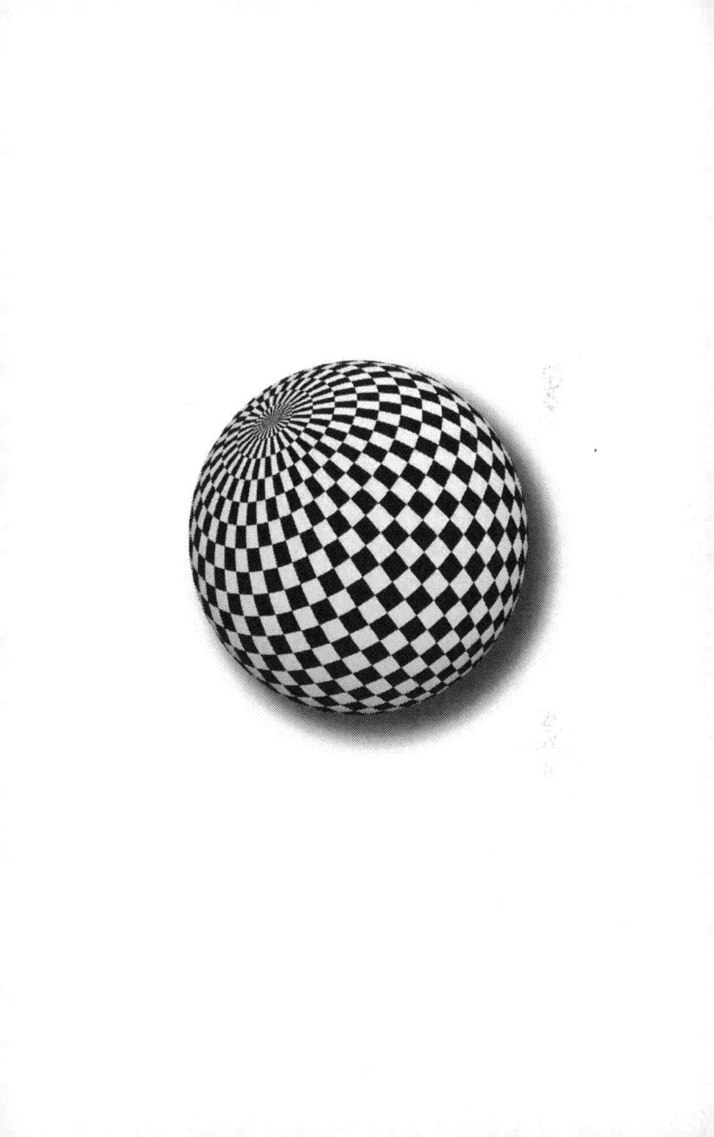

I never act out of desperation,
except when I absolutely have to.

I try to be sincere in all situations,
but especially when I don't mean it.

Total fulfillment just isn't
doing it for me anymore.

Keep shedding childhood fantasies that aren't serving you anymore, until all that's left is a unicorn in the garden.

I now place 100% of my faith in pure, scientific reasoning.

My Zodiac sign is the one that doesn't believe in astrology.

I'm still sprawled on the ground wrestling
with whether I'm my own worst enemy.

When teaching my students
about non-linear mathematics,
I always start at the beginning.

I've been too busy pulling
my own head out of my own ass to inquire
how your colonoscopy went last week.

Heraclitus said the Universe is in constant flux in 400 BC, and things haven't changed much since then.

❂

We all have to bend the facts a little in life to compensate for how we distort reality.

❂

I now only trust the opinions of people who admit they probably don't know what the hell is going on.

EPILOGUE

Life comes down to three things:
enjoying the pleasures of the Earth,
marveling at the mysteries of the Cosmos,
and catching whoever's
using your dumpster.

~CHAPTER 14~

The Power of Later

"If quantum mechanics hasn't profoundly shocked you, you haven't understood it yet."
— Niels Bohr

"You're no bigger than the things that annoy you."
— Jerry Bundsen

"I do random acts of kindness every four hours - usually somewhere here in the neighborhood."
— Gregg Eisenberg

I can't make cheap excuses for myself
because frankly I just don't have the time.

A little bit of unhappiness on your part has
gone a long way in tempering other
people's jealousy.

I sometimes feel inadequate,
but I can't even do *that* right.

In this moment you're the oldest you've ever been, the youngest you'll ever be, and the least medicated I've seen you quite a while.

Just because you spent many years repeating a mistake doesn't mean you can't go out and try to make new ones.

I've finally mastered my control issues; now I'm going to master yours.

Too much dogma in the news
is making us all catatonic.

If it weren't for the pharmaceuticals I'm
taking, I'd still be using drugs.

I think my own thoughts every second,
feel my own emotions every minute,
and drink the Kool-Aid every hour.

Krishnamurti wrote: "It is a sign of poor health to be well-adjusted to a sick society", and I'm sure glad I don't have *that* problem.

Reminders about the true
empty nature of reality
are pounding me from all directions today.

It appears that the world is just an illusion,
but things might not be what they seem.

I am not running away from the truth,
but I *am* backing up slowly.

I love that you're so dynamic
and I hope you never change.

I passed my geometry class
in a parallel universe.

The theory that we evolved from monkeys
makes a lot of people howl in disbelief!

⊛

The bible basically proves that sibling rivalry
is healthy for our survival (because only
the weakest ones get sold into slavery.)

⊛

Imagining God has eternal love for me
is really no substitute
for a great dinner party.

Impermanence looks like it is going
to be around a long, long time…

It's obvious that we are all completely alone:
just look into the billions of human eyes.

I take 100% responsibility for my actions
every time the opportunity
happens to roll around.

I am learning how to be less co-dependent,
and it's for your own good.

Voltaire wrote, "Don't drop my name
just to sell more books"
(but my agent sees it differently.)

Take the road of moderation
as far as you can, I say,
and never look back!

A little bit of understatement always
goes a helluva long way.

One of the most effective ways to improve
things, in terms of immediate results,
is to stop trying to make them better.

I'm not defensive about all my ideas;
just the ones I'm not too sure about.

I'm trying to reinvent myself
as someone who got it right the first time.

If you stop to help others along the way,
you'll never reach enlightenment.

⊛

Your egotistical pride is the only thing
standing between you and eternal greatness.

⊛

I want to become a boddhisatva
in *this* lifetime, and when I do,
I'm taking all you shmucks with me.

EPILOGUE

The moment I grasped the Taoist concept
of "effortlessly following things
the way they naturally are,"
I knew I had to change my
whole outlook and personality.

~CHAPTER 15~

Seek And Ye Shall Look For

"The key to happiness is having a large, loving, caring, close-knit family in another city."
— George Burns

"I only have one regret in life: that I wasn't someone else."
— Woody Allen

"The best part is, all this misery didn't cost me a thing!"
— Gregg Eisenberg

We have all been put here to confront our aloneness, and others have been put here to help.

If we didn't need to be accepted by the group so much, we might not be so nice to each other.

We've all got to be as fierce as warriors to endure how completely powerless we truly are.

I'm trying to tell the Universe something,
but it just isn't ready for the lesson yet.

⊛

Believing there are "no accidents in life"
was my first big mistake.

⊛

Knowing how perfectly free from suffering
we could all be is what pains me the most.

A life of always wanting more
is good enough for me!

❂

Try to be less driven in life
and appreciate the simple things more.
Now, do it again, faster!

❂

I'm detached from my thoughts, detached
from my emotions, and, at the moment,
separated from my wife and kid.

I use 72% of my mental capacity thinking
about sex; the rest of it I just waste.

❂

I achieved heightened self-awareness at a
young age, long before I even realized it.

❂

The new app for protecting yourself
from corporate brainwashing is free,
if you sign up for Amazon Prime today.

I respect myself enough to seek validation
from only the most prestigious
members of society.

There is an awful lot to be said about
non-verbal communication,
but I can't listen to it right now.

If you can't be authentic with others,
at least offer your pretenses sincerely.

Special relativity proved that if you are
running towards me at a constant speed,
and then shine a flashlight in my direction,
I should run the hell away.

⊛

Total randomness doesn't always work
the way you hope it does.

⊛

I just wasn't meant
to be a fatalist.

The truth is very simple;
nothing isn't ambiguous.

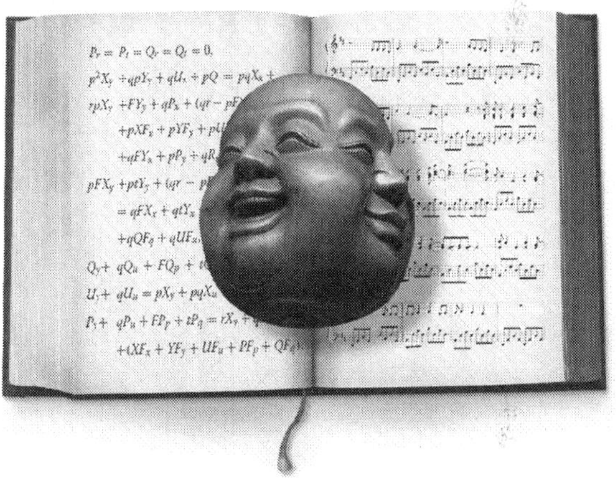

$P_r = P_t = Q_r = Q_t = 0,$
$p^2X_y + qpY_y + qU_y + pQ = pqX_x +$
$rpX_y + FY_y + qP_x + (qr - pF$
$+pXF_x + pYF_y + p$
$+qFY_x + pP_y + qR$
$pFX_y + ptY_y + (qr - p$
$= qFX_r + qtY_x$
$+qQF_q + qUF_u$
$Q_y + qQ_u + FQ_p +$
$U_y + qU_u = pX_y + pqX_u$
$P_y + qP_u + FP_p + tP_q = rX_y +$
$+(XF_x + YF_y + UF_u + PF_p + QF_q$

Once I start resorting to positive thinking,
I know I'm already swimming upstream.

The last thing I need to do
to feel complete in life is to
stop putting more conditions on it.

Managing my expectations didn't improve
my life nearly as much as I believed it would.

Many doctors mistake "healthy exurberance" for "manic illness" (and I'm delighted to be proving all of them wrong!)

⊛

What a relief it was to find out we were being radically paranoid over nothing.

⊛

We were courageous enough to nervously endure our overwhelming fear.

I'm willing to go to great lengths to show
the world I'm done trying to prove myself.

I wandered far and wide to avoid
straying from my critical path.

24 million chemical reactions happen in my
body every 15 seconds, and you're asking
how I've been the past few *weeks*??

In order to really "seize the day" today,
I'll need to "put some things off"
until tomorrow.

⊛

My neo-cortex wants to forgive you, but my
reptiliain brain-stem is deciding this one.

⊛

When it comes to drinking and smoking,
I'm taking a little break from doing without.

EPILOGUE

We're not physical beings
having a spiritual experience,
nor are we spiritual beings
having a physical experience;
we're on hold with Comcast.

~CHAPTER 16~

The Beginning Is Near

"People can only be happy when they do not assume that the object of life is happiness."
— George Orwell

"I don't deserve this award, but I have arthritis and I don't deserve that either."
— Jack Benny

"I really should have stopped regretting the past a long time ago."
— Gregg Eisenberg

Suffering is such an intrinsic part of the human experience, seems we should all try to enjoy it more.

Happiness is not a destination, but you probably haven't arrived at that conclusion yet.

When will we finally wake up from the myth that we are still somehow asleep?

Transcending the illusion of ego was easy;
what's hard is not bragging about it.

⊛

I'm desperately driven by my need not to be
controlled by any pathology.

⊛

I'm lucky my blog about
the end of civilization was published
before the internet went up in smoke.

Most people need to be told what's
good and bad, and who am I to say
if that's right or wrong?

It's very comforting to reassure myself that
I'm not just telling myself the stories
I want to hear.

The moral of the allegory is that life is
not a fairy tale.

The Universe keeps telling me that I'm not hearing voices on a vast enough scale.

⊛

Things never really were
the way they used to be,
but I hope someday they will.

⊛

The internet has brought us all much
closer and closer to realizing how
far apart we truly are.

Were they not so vain about their looks,
humans would be the most beautiful
of all living creatures.

If you'd just admit that I'm right, I would
immediately open up to your point of view.

Once I liberated my mind from
the limitations of Aristotelian logic,
everything started making sense.

I'm a lifelong learner:
I make new mistakes all the time.

❀

I don't let other people set my standards
any more than most people do.

❀

It took a lot of misery to be this happy.

I have finally boiled my philosophy down to
"Everything is boundless."

It now takes our species two entire decades
of nurturing our offspring
to prepare them for one more decade
of living in the basement.

It takes an entire village to raise a child,
but only one dipstick to know the oil is low.

Love thine enemies
(and then work your way up to family.)

Consciousness is the greatest mystery of science, but most people are completely in the dark about this.

Einstein insisted God does not play dice with the Universe, and I'm betting everything I own on this.

I agree the rise and fall of humankind is epic in its overall scale and design – and your side o' fries'll be right up!

I don't engage in the cult of celebrity worship, and according to *Newsweek* neither does Denzel Washington.

If God is watching me,
He obviously hasn't heard of Netflix.

We are already omniscient;
we just don't know it yet.

Parmenides taught that "reality is totally immutable" in 400 BC, and nothing's been the same since.

⊛

I now have a big-picture, panoramic view on how fragmented everything truly is.

⊛

If we only knew now
what we're about to find out....

Other than being chained to the human condition, all things are possible.

Our collective destination is unknown, and something tells me we should keep it that way as long as possible.

It doesn't matter
where you've lived in the world;
what matters is what's still alive in you.

I'm using my remaining adult years to cultivate childlike wonder at the Universe.

❁

I'll become the ideal person I'm ultimately meant to be as soon as I'm good and done being who I am.

❁

I'll always remember this moment together, whatever your name is.

EPILOGUE

Life isn't always about
what's going to happen next
(which you're about to find out.)

ABOUT THE AUTHOR

Gregg Eisenberg is a stand-up philosopher living in Boulder, Colorado. He grew up writing poems in a Jewish household in Chicagoland where he learned how to feel a dissonant mixture of awkwardness and confidence about himself from some of the most loving people you could ever meet. When his childhood peers went off to Dartmouth, he went on an experimental writing journey across the deserts of Greece, Turkey, Syria, Jordan, Palestine, and Israel. At the time he told his mother: "I'm a poet - anything else is extra."

After months of circulating through dangerous countries and scribbling notes in remote border towns, he received an auspicious fortune cookie in a Chinese restaurant in the Arab quarter of Jerusalem with a scarcely-known quote from the ancient Chinese philosopher *Lao-Tzu*. This sparked his fascination with eastern thought and led him to study Asian language and literature at the University of California. There the coastal ecosystems and exposure to Taoist thought further riveted his imagination and forced him to take his exploration of aesthetics (and restless mind-syndrome) further. Songwriting became his passion, in a genre he calls **Heavy Meadow**. After working in China and then completing a Master's in Geography at Boston University, Gregg moved to Colorado to continue writing music and work to protect the west's fragile environments.

Gregg formed **Curved-Space Comedy** in 2016 and under that name performs his multi-media, science-comedy show **Even the Earth is Bipolar** in planetariums, publishes his books, and provides private speaking events. In 2018, he released two titles: **Letting Go Is All We Have to Hold Onto: Humor for Humans**, and **Love Without Madness (Amor Sin Locura)** - bilingual poetry which he performs with live musical accompaniment. In a somewhat radical return to his roots, he is currently writing **Follow Your Bris** to perform in synagogues, house parties, and smoky lounges around America.

"The desire to spread levity in the world
weighs heavily upon me." – Gregg Eisenberg

(For information about the fortune in the cookie,
contact Curved-Space Comedy.)

Humor: www.curvedspacecomedy.com
Music: www.heavymeadow.org
Poetry: www.lovewithoutmadness.com

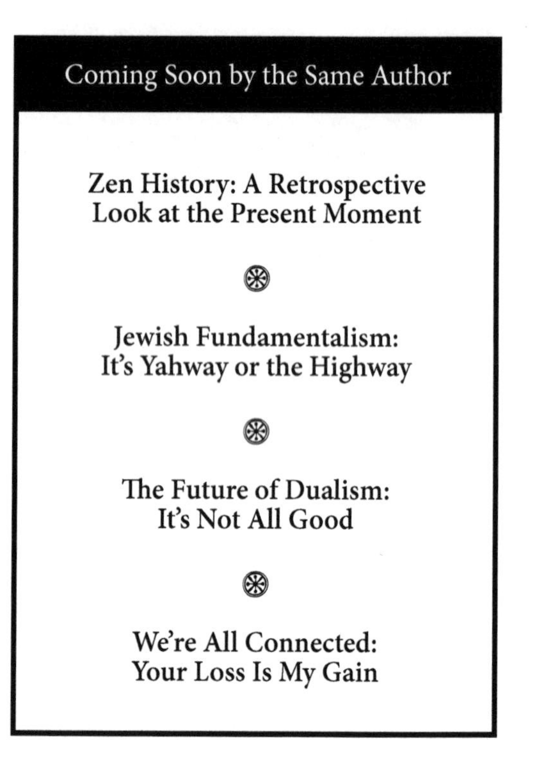
Coming Soon by the Same Author
Zen History: A Retrospective Look at the Present Moment
Jewish Fundamentalism: It's Yahway or the Highway
The Future of Dualism: It's Not All Good
We're All Connected: Your Loss Is My Gain

36500120R00160

Made in the USA
Lexington, KY
15 April 2019